THE GOD OF
LONELINESS

THE GOD OF LONELINESS

POEMS

Charles K. Carter

REBEL SATORI PRESS
NEW ORLEANS & NEW YORK

Published in the United States of America by
Rebel Satori Press
www.rebelsatoripress.com

Cover Art: Jonathan Kent Adams, *Self* (2013-2014, 22x28in).

Paperback ISBN: 978-1-60864-339-4

Contents

Barter

Airport Musings   1

Flying in Dreamland   2

On the Playground   4

One Last Polka   5

Howl   7

Murder in Dreamland   8

Linger   11

In Response to *Alex* (Pencil & Oil Pastels, 2007)   12

Paper Fortune Teller   13

The Journal   14

Drinking   17

In the Shadows   18

Homophobia in Dreamland   19

Safety Check   22

Big Death   23

Christening   24

Roadtrippin' in Dreamland   25

Petals   27

Quarantine Lover   28

Anything But   29

Headlights   30

Cloudy Fragments (Notes App After Hookup on May 3, 2022)   31

His Holy Trinity

(And He Says, "Oh God")   35

Ghosting   36

Budding   37

Report to the Mothership   38
Apocalypse in Dreamland   40
On Creation   42
A Way Through   45
Resuscitation   49
Lit in Dreamland   50
Roadside Assistance   51
Lovebirds in Dreamland   52
Just in Case   54
Someplace Beautiful   55
To Be Seen   56
Drought   58
Emergency Exit   59
Pop Quiz   60
Extraction   62
Drowning in Dreamland   64
Zombie   67
In the Company of Ghosts   68
Mourning the Dead Cat   70
Atlas of Longing   72
Acknowledgments   74
About the Author   76

& I guess loneliness is another type of debt
& there is no cure for the ache
– Hanif Abdurraqib

Barter

A crow fashions a nest of shiny aluminum foil scraps to blind a
 mate to fulfill his urges.

A dog trades tricks for a treat.

A little boy collects golf balls for a quarter each at the country
 club.

His sister trades candy for paints to better tell her story when
 her vocabulary just doesn't cut it.

The farmer trades a goat for seeds.

The teens trade dares for kisses.

A ticket is needed for a ride.

I learned to barter my labor for Melissa Etheridge concert
 tickets.

A handjob for a drink.

A book for advice.

A credit line or two for an escape.

I bought a cat for company.

Picked up a man for better company.

Adopted a dog for even better company.

But I would trade it all for you.

You know who you are.

I

Airport Musings

Do not leave baggage unattended.
Unattended baggage will be confiscated.

Someone please take my baggage.
Let me lay my trauma down and walk away.

Send in the bomb squad to come in and obliterate
my body issues and my daddy issues and this anxiety.

Blow this self-doubt to smithereens
and I'll rise like a 747.

Flying in Dreamland

& i was so confused.

i was riding on the back of a flying golf cart
with my parents who were preparing to renew their vows.
& it was strange
because they have been divorced for five years.
& i don't think this could ever happen
because she thinks he is an abusive asshole
& he thinks she's a whore.
& how can you renew vows
if you're not even married.

& he kept singing "this thing called love"
& i had never heard him sing this song before
& i have never heard him listen to this song
or talk about queen
or freddie mercury at all
& he was actually good
& my mom was swooning
& i was feeling nauseous.

& we were flying
through the air on this flying golf cart
& my dad was mistaking
my tears of frustration for tears of joy.
& we went by some huge garbage dump
for the city of los angeles
& then we flew past these huge trees

with huge swarms of bald eagles
& their nests
& i began to slip from the golf cart
& i asked him to slow down.
& they both just laughed at me
& called me a faggot
& i wanted to jump.

On the Playground

You put me on the merry-go-'round
and spun me 'round faster and faster.

I wanted off but you said to hold on,
to take a breath and ease into the discomfort,

that I would soon feel alive.
And I did.

I felt dizzy in your ecstasy
and then it all slowed down.

One final push
and your laughter lingered, haunting me.

I jerked furiously from side to side
but I couldn't see you in the spiraling landscape.

I had to drag my feet in the dirt and gravel.
I had to scuff up my new tennis shoes

to stop spinning in your direction.
I can still taste your dust in my mouth.

One Last Polka

When I visit my great-grandma,
she usually doesn't know who I am.
Sometimes she thinks I am my uncle.
Last week, she thought I was her brother.
Before that, she thought I was my father.

They say not to correct someone with dementia,
that destroying their delusion could lead to an episode.
So I smile and nod and play that part of whoever
she thinks I am on any given day.

I smile and nod as she asks me
if I can absolve her of her sins.
I'm not sure if it's because I'm wearing all black
but she thinks I am a priest today.
And though I am far from holy,
I take her sins upon me and forgive her every transgression.
She beams like heaven is within her reach.

I smile and nod as she asks my great-grandpa
why he left her here, why he hasn't called,
why he hasn't taken her out dancing.
She misses dancing.
So I pull up polka music on my iPhone
and dance with her in her wheelchair.
She beams like heaven is in her eyes.

After her spirit has left her body,

I lean in and whisper that I love her.
I wonder who she thought was holding her hand and saying
   goodbye.
Who did she think I was in that moment?
Did she know it was the real me
or did she just think I was a child who never came to visit?

Howl

My father had a tendency
to buy a new pet every three-to-six months
and when their newness wore off,

he'd kick them around or neglect them.
For a few years while growing up,
we had a bloodhound.

She never got much for attention.
She was young and full of sexual energy,
howling night after night

for a little doggy company,
for a little warmth in her cold outdoor enclosure;
until one night she ended up with a bullet between her eyes.

I'm not entirely sure my father didn't do it,
jealous of her vitality
and eager to play victim of such a loss.

When I approached tender teenhood
with a queer, lustful howl beginning to blossom in my throat,
I knew I needed to break my chains and run

or end up just the same.

Murder in Dreamland

& my mother accidentally killed my brother
when he pushed her last buttons.
he pushed her up the stairs
so she pushed him down
& with a smack
his head hit the concrete.
& he was gone.
& she didn't want to go to jail
& it was all an accident
but in a panic she hoisted him into the basement deep freeze
& placed all the boxes of christmas gifts on top.
she sat in a corner
& cried until
i came to visit
& found her there.

& she told me the truth.

& i didn't know what to do.
i understood my brother's anger
& how he pushed people to the edge.
& i didn't want my mom to end up in prison
so i kept her secret
though i had no advice.

soon
she told my sister
& our father

& my other brother
& a plan was hatched
to bury him in the woods
behind the country club.
it all made me uneasy
but they called me too sensitive
& told me to push it all down
& to help lift the body into the trunk of the suv.
& we transported him in broad daylight
& by *we* i mean *them*
because i chickened out
& i couldn't ride in the same car as his body
as they took him to his final resting place.
& i thought of how my brother's children would never know
where their father was laid to rest
& i thought about how disrespectful that was
& i went to buy a pack of cigarettes
& i lit up after five years of not smoking.

& i thought the nightmare was over
but a week later my mom choked out my other brother.

& he was gone too.

& there was an elaborate plan
for his burial at this rental by the lake
& again
i was told to hush my sadness
& sensitivity
& just go with the plan
& enjoy the nice vacation

& i was a bad son
for making my mom feel any guiltier.

& i hid in the closet
& cried thinking about my brother's laughter
& my sister came in looking for a shirt
& she ignored me
& i wondered
if my body would be next
to find its way to an unmarked grave.

Linger

I am not one to look in the mirror often but when I do,
I am drawn to checking out my own nose
because this drunk guy
I fooled around with once in high school
told me I had the perfect nose.

He literally stroked it, admired it,
and complimented it for ten minutes
before going down on me.

I look in the mirror now
and wonder about what he said,
how much of his lingering words were true.
He also said he loved me that night before asking me out.

We've never officially broken up and I am a sucker for the details.

In Response to *Alex* (Pencil & Oil Pastels, 2007)

My grandma wanted a piece of artwork I created,
a moody surreal drawing of the first man I loved
colored in warm tones, his orange and red-hot body
staring at a cool blue-violet reflection.

She thinks it's a self-portrait.
I guess in a way she's right,
his hot blood staring at my cold cold core.
No wonder he couldn't love me.

Whenever I come to visit,
while she always has to pack me a bag of groceries
from her bargain-bought overstocked overstuffed pantry,
while she throws in jars of peanut butter and expired snack cakes,

all I can see is the first man I loved staring me down,
the grown man who told me he loved me
but never let me grow up
so I could grow warm in his gaze.

Paper Fortune Teller

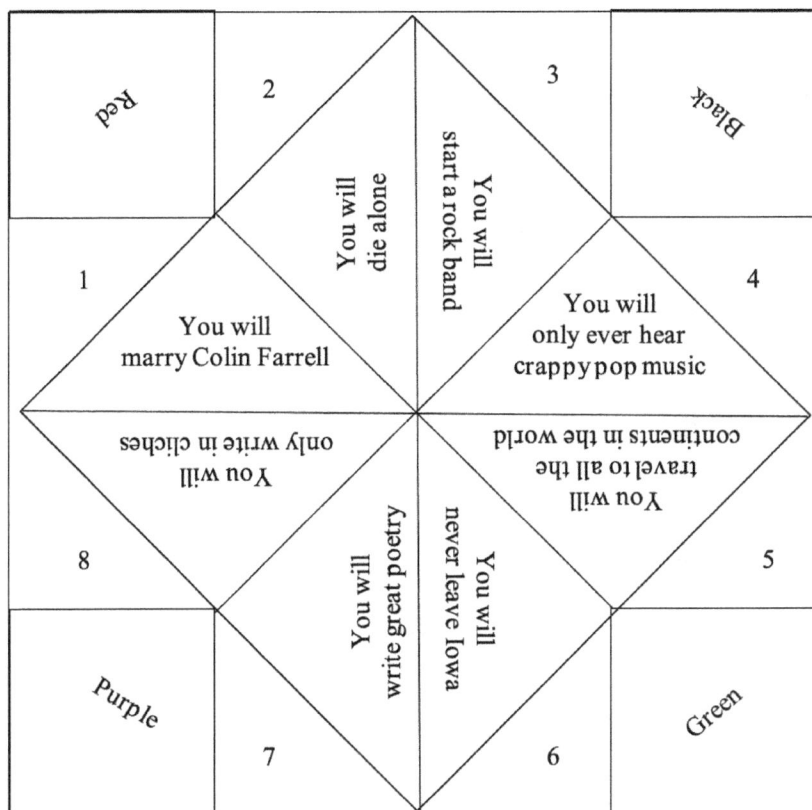

Red

2

3

Black

You will
die alone

You will
start a rock band

1

You will
marry Colin Farrell

You will
only ever hear
crappy pop music

4

You will
only write in cliches

You will
travel to all the
continents in the world

8

You will
write great poetry

You will
never leave Iowa

5

Purple

7

6

Green

13

The Journal

I found a spiral notebook with a yellow cover from back in my high school days. The front was titled *Tales of a Gay, Left-Handed, Monophobic, Vegetarian Trying to Find a Place in this Shitty World: Volume 1.* The back was covered in heartagrams and peace signs and written inside was a self-penned attempt at autogenic training:

Stop breathing	Stop seeing
Stop seeing	Stop seeing
Stop seeing	Stop seeing
Stop seeing	Stop seeing
Stop hearing	Stop hearing
Stop hearing	Stop hearing
Stop breathing	Stop breathing
Stop caring	Stop breathing
Stop caring	Stop caring
Stop caring	Stop caring
	Stop caring

I used to try this all the time but it never took. It never worked. Here I am, working on *Volume 16.* Seeing. Hearing. Breathing. And I'm still caring way too goddamn much.

II

Drinking

Sometimes
I look across the bar
and I can't help but think
of the rows of Siamese fighting fish at the supermarket,
each in their little solitary, plastic jars
– hungry with lust, jumpy with anger,
ready to fight, ready to fuck,
ready to kill any male who threatens his seed,
ready to protect oneself at all costs;
it's what their genetics have trained them to do.
This is what we are all trained to do:
Fight. Survive. Be the last one standing.

In the Shadows

Meet me in the shadows of the checkerboard
created by these dim parking lot lights.
We can hide here in the hushed darkness
and make out all night.

We can dream of getting our own place
or driving away from it all hand-in-hand,
becoming refugees seeking sanctuary
in the soft Arizona sands.

Homophobia in Dreamland

& i wanted to be in
& out
& back on the road in five minutes
or less.
i went pee
& then thumbed through the energy bars
& trail mixes before making a selection
& going for a fountain soda.
some sugar
& caffeine
would make the last 2.5 hours of this trip go by a little easier.

& there was some dude at the fountain
who noticed my rainbow melissa etheridge pride t-shirt
& said gays *don't get no service here.*

we don't deserve a refuel?
i laughed
& tried to brush past him
but he got pushy
& adamant
& the store clerk tried to intervene
but he kept getting in the way
& getting more
& more
aggressive.
the veins on his red neck began to pop.
& soon she threatened to call the cops

& he said to do it
that god was always on his side
no matter what the *ungodly* liberal laws of the land say.

& she kept trying to step in
but he wouldn't let me pass
& he kept trying to get me to repent for my ways.

& she told him the cops were on the way
& all of a sudden
he wanted to pay for his shit
but he did it obnoxiously slow
so that she couldn't serve me.
he stood guard until the sirens got closer.
& then he bolted out the door.

here, she winked,
handing me a twenty.
this is on him.
he forgot his cash back.
maybe you should get some lube
or a cher cd
or something ungodly.
she laughed.

& i wanted to laugh
& move on
but homophobia in dreamland
is as real
& scary
as it is

in the waking
land of the free.

Safety Check

They say if you live in Arizona
that you should shine a blacklight
around your home to check for scorpions.
You should check corners and cupboards, closets
and cowboy boots and underneath your bed.

But when I do the blacklight check,
I only discover dusty footprints from where he walked
out the door for good.
I keep scrubbing and scrubbing
but they remain.

I get to the point
where I stop using the blacklight
and I hope for some venom
to remedy
this ache.

Big Death

They call an orgasm *little death*
so I decide if I want to go
I should cum while I do it –
kick the chair out from underneath myself
as the jizz starts to throb and spasm
towards the edge of light,
let my life force fly free
as I exit this world
cock in hand,
rope snapping my neck quick
like a chicken about to be plucked,
carved up, and broasted for Sunday dinner.

Christening

A single road can have many names:

> Interstate 35
> Avenue of the Saints
> 34th Infantry Division Highway
> Purple Heart Trail
> Monarch Highway

And I wonder what names you might hold for me:

> beloved
> flirt
> trickster
> disaster
> wound

And, I too, contain multitudes.

Roadtrippin' in Dreamland

& we picked up our rental car
at the seattle airport.
it reeked of pot
so you called it the weed wagon.

& we searched for license plates for all the states.
we drove north to anacortes to watch the whales.
when we hydroplaned going 80 mph
our hearts jumped simultaneously.

& in oregon we enjoyed a fire on the beach.
the seabirds begged for your breakfast
as you sat on the patio
& talked to your mom
while he gave me head on the hotel bed.

& we all peed in the redwood forest.
& i, being so gay that i don't know pussy or cars,
misread a sign to keep a lookout for a white volvo
as vulva.
you both wouldn't let me live that down.

& we watched the sunset in san francisco
& we hiked in big sur
& we smoked weed at venice beach
& we drank champagne
& watched an endless pod of dolphins swim by at san clemente
          state park.

we ended the trip with only missing three states in our license plate game.

Petals

The goat eats the flower
not because it tastes good
but because it looks good.

He wanders around
and eats pretty things
because he wants them to be

all his own.

Quarantine Lover

They say you shed
an outer layer of skin
every two weeks
so when the experts said
to stay at home,
we made a love nest
and as we exercised
and played cards
and ate breakfast in bed,
I became refreshed,
became new again! and again! and
again and again! and again and
again and again and again! and –

But as soon
as the city opened up,
he fled
and now I can't eat maple syrup
without the memory of his erect nipples
and I can't look at the Uno deck
without imagining his smug winning face.
And I am surrounded
by eight ghosts of him
floating around this empty apartment,
wishing they would become whole
and hold me once again.

Anything But

I have walls full of art and memorabilia that no one ever comes over to see. The guest bed is mostly cat hair because she's the only one who has slept there in the last three years.

I stopped taking my antidepressants because I don't want to become dependent upon them to level out.

I have shelves full of books as if these strangers' stories could cure my loneliness or my fear of dying. I am sure I can learn more from a book than any outing in this podunk fucking town.

I stopped taking the strawberry-flavored edibles I smuggled in the trunk of my ex-boyfriend's car from the next state over.

I have had the same bottle of wine my grandma gave me for my book release ten and a half months ago. I'm afraid if I start to drink alone that I won't stop until I drown myself while trying to become a mermaid.

I stopped thinking about you when I masturbate because what's the point if it'll never come true? I jizz in the condoms that have been left in my nightstand drawer to expire. Easy cleanup gives them some use. I wonder what my use is anymore.

Some days I want to leave this life. I want to flee from this red state. I want to abandon this red family. I want to burn down this old house and collect the insurance money so I can travel and write for a while. I want to leave this crumbling democracy. I want to float in the sea or be swallowed by those fluffy kaleidoscope clouds. I want to become a circle, a square, a star, or a hexagon. I want to become a shape instead of a color, anything but this blue.

Headlights

When driving at night,
mailboxes begin to look like deer.
Reflectors in the ditches look like eyes.

The silhouettes of shrubs look like kangaroos
and flamingos and you.
I'm always trying to find you.

Cloudy Fragments (Notes App After Hookup on May 3, 2022)

He admits to getting fucked up again. He said the other day it took him an hour and a half to walk the six blocks to work because he thought if he moved too fast his heart might explode all over the pavement.

He smokes a menthol while I stroke his bare thigh. He can't look me in the eyes. He can't bear to be seen. Instead, he thumbs through the apps on his phone, looking at messages and photos from other guys on Messenger and Grindr and Bumble and –

I fuck him anyway because it's not like anyone else wants this portly body.

Afterwards, he cries in my arms about wanting love and he says that maybe he should give it a try with a guy who drugged him and blackmailed him. He tries to convince my quiet stare that the guy *really is nice deep down*. He's fucked up like we all are. He's convincing himself that maybe he should move in with this guy.

Maybe we all feel like our hearts are going to beat out of our chests as we stumble towards something that might make us feel whole. Is that what love is? *I don't know.* Is that the root of addiction? *Probably.* Are they the same thing? *You tell me.*

III

His Holy Trinity (And He Says, "Oh God")

after Allen Ginsberg

BLESS HIS HOLY COCK

BLESS HIS HOLY ASSHOLE

BLESS HIS HOLY HANDS

The same two fingers I use to do the sign of the cross
are now thrusting inside of him
while he bends down
panting tongues
in my ear.

He is riding me as I stroke his cock until he sprays
on me like holy water on Palm Sunday,
blessing me with
his sacred
salt.

His Adam's apple pressed against my palm
feels like a rosary bead, feels like passion
folded into prayer, lifted up to
a god of desire and
longing.

Ghosting

What an appropriate term that is
for when a man has a hold of you
though you never actually see him.
What an appropriate label
for a man who listens to me spill my guts
but never opens himself up to me.
He always leaves my gut-spills on read.
He's a man whose touch feels like it's always just out of reach
but close enough to make the hair on my neck rise.
Here I am stuck somewhere between anger and bargaining
and I still see him in flashes of teeth and knuckles and eyelashes.

Budding

And I swallow these seeds down down down,
waiting for love or something like it to bud in my stomach,
stems to rise through my ribcage,

flower petals to bloom,
to pump fragrant flowery perfume into my heart
and through these tributaries some call veins.

But he never returned to nourish with his warmth.
He never returned my texts or postcards,
my nude photographs or want ads searching only for him.

These seeds dried up and any sign of life withered
in the desert that continues to expand inside my stomach.
Someday, it will be famous, more vast than the Sahara.

Report to the Mothership

These humans have wild imaginations
that sometimes lead them in the right direction.
They accidentally create computers and apps,
genetically engineered food items and bombs.
Their writers depict alien worlds
and alien technologies
and sometimes,
by mere accident, I'm sure,
they get something right
 – or well, almost.

In the sci-fi comedy film series, *Men in Black*,
the detectives have, with the help of their extraterrestrial friends,
developed a tool to wipe a human's memory in the flash of a pen.
A pen will do but
we can impart these powers on many ordinary objects.
I keep a keychain-sized Etch-a-Sketch on hand
whenever I need to erase a human's mind.

I never slip up
and reveal my true identity
but sometimes I fall too deep for a human
and need to back things up a bit,
erase their memories
of my heart-spillings
or tongue-fillings.
Somedays,
I wish I could smash this little toy,

let its sand scatter on the pavement
and with it spill out all my feelings
and true colors: green and red and full of heart.

Apocalypse in Dreamland

& guns
& horror movie masks
make it to the concert venue
where you are there
to see your favorite rock band
& all of a sudden the apocalypse is upon you.
& there are gridlocks
& blackouts
& total chaos.

& people are stealing cars
& you steal a boat
to get through the river seine.
& rich men are eating lobster
& veal
as if nothing is going wrong
& the rich are not very adaptive
to changing their routines.
& everyone is hoarding resources.
& you run into a hostage situation
& you outwit the vigilante group
who is run by a narcissist promising salvation
in making the apocalypse great again
& he says that everyone is out to get them
though his people
are the only ones bashing people's heads with hammers
& breaking the kneecaps
of volunteer community peace officers who are monitoring the

streets.

& you hitch a ride from your uncle by marriage
& his kids didn't make it
so he treats you like a son
& he is going to take you to your husband
who is at their house on the edge of this city.
& it's been days since you've seen him
& you've been waiting for a reminder
of what he tastes like
because days are like eons
in the apocalyptic calendar.
& your aunt has a job for you
helping out at her diner at the edge of the city.
& the edge of civilization has the most humanity these days.

& there's a stray dog in your bed
because your man needed something warm to keep your place
something warm – just in case.

On Creation

i.

along the riverbed
where jesse
and a beautiful stranger once
swapped head
in his ex's car

jesse now cracks open
his lobster chest
pulls his heart-
strings
apart
and rolls one in the red river clay

creating a bronze boy
with longing eyes
and sharp teeth.

for a while the two are always seen
zig-zagging up and down c-38
holding hands and singing spanish love songs
with the windows down.

but within a month
his hard bronze boy
decides he wants to see the world.

the creator holds
his creation's hand
begging him not to go.

but something hard and clay
is always able to break away
and jesse is left alone again
with only a red clay hand
to sit in the passenger seat.

ii.

after reading piles of greek myths
and drinking his weight in whiskey
jesse decides to try again.
he can create something better:
a man who will stay
who will not be drawn to passion but logic
and so he thanks the cute waiter
with a wink and a smile

and he takes a hammer to his own skull
and pulls out a mannequin
who looks just like the cute waiter
and he breathes life into him with a kiss
and he postures the shiny legs into an ideal position

and they make love
once before the mannequin runs away
too smart to stick with a self-destructive lovesick fool
too cerebral to fall
for fairytales of monogamy
and shared checking accounts.

jesse climbs the mountain of his solitude
made from the relics of these failed love(r)s
he cries lightning bolts and he *is* a god – the god of loneliness.

A Way Through

My therapist keeps trying to get me to visualize
my broken adult self giving my younger child self
the love he needs to heal.
She seems to think that this will help me find the self-love
that I am missing after decades of conditioned self-hate.
I have a hard time suspending reality for this fantastical medicine
        show,
this capsule of snake oil to heal all that ails me.
Is this really supposed to work or is it merely a placebo?

While walking a nature trail,
I came across a fallen archway constructed of recycled pipes,
cardboard decorated with splatter paint, foam flowers,
and a skunk-pattern feather headdress.
A handwritten posterboard sign beside it says:
Imagine what you want the most,
walk through this portal
and you will find what you're looking for.
If the arch was standing,
maybe my desperate heart would have given it a shot.

Instead, I keep seeking out a portal
that is inside of another man's body.
His mouth to give me the softness that I need.
His eyes a mirror to reflect what I give to him.
I can call this self-love,
can't I?

IV

Resuscitation

I was a record, baby,
but you were the needle,
pressing into my grooves,
making me crackle,
making me sing.

Lit in Dreamland

& we got really high
& started with the laughing fits
& i couldn't see through the laughing tears
& our dog ran away
but she came back riding in on the back of an orca
& she's named stevie
after stevie nicks
& she rode in on an orca
with a black fringy shawl around her neck
& a tambourine in her paw
& she sang about losing her daddies
but here we are stevie
& here we are
& here we are
& won't you sing "gold dust woman"
for us once again?

Roadside Assistance

Somewhere south of Keokuk,
we picnic below a bridge on Sugar Creek.

We feed each other whole-grain crackers
and grapes and share a cigarette.

He puts both his hands on my heart and says,
This is mine. Please, take care of it for me.

Lovebirds in Dreamland

& the first place we met was in my apartment
the grungy one with my secondhand broken couch
that smelled like sex
& marlboro reds.

& then we stayed at your place a lot
where your cousin got fucked by strangers in your bathroom.
where we first fucked.
where you'd sneak out to smoke weed
& pop pills with the neighbors.
where we spent christmas quietly fucking
while your cousin slept a few feet away from us
on the couch of your studio apartment.

& then we had a place where we lived on the edge of town.
a mockingbird sang outside the office window
& we took in a cat
& named it anastasia beaverhausen
before we realized she had testicles
but we kept the name.
& you were chased by cartoon zombies
& when we moved
you took a sharpie
& wrote our initials in a heart
inside the bedroom closet.

& we ran out of gas money on our move
but we made it eventually by pirate ship.

& we crashed with three different family members
until we got our new apartment
next to the bars where we could always hear the drunks singing
& fighting with those plastic sporks from taco bell.

& then we had another apartment.

& then we bought our first house.
& now we are preparing to pack up
& move across the country
with no jobs.
only hope
& i wonder
if that's enough to get by on
& i wonder
if we will survive this empty ache in our bones.

.

Just in Case

I keep having dreams where he dies
so every night I anxiously lie awake
listening in case he might stop breathing.

To feel like I have control of the situation,
I have started to collect his breath
in zip-lock bags and mason jars

and empty plastic grocery sacks.
If there comes a day when
his breath does cease,

I will have his life
to shove back into his lungs.

Someplace Beautiful

I asked him to move across the country with me to someplace where we knew no one, where we had no jobs or housing or friends or ex-boyfriends or other connections, someplace that is simply beautiful.

I've always said I would never kill myself because I am too afraid of death. If I think too much about it, I quickly spiral into a wave of panic. But the more I walk amongst these ancient trees, the more I realize I do not belong to this world.

I asked him to move somewhere beautiful so that when I finally gather the courage to die, it will be in someplace that is dew-dropped and moss-soft and he will be in someplace with great splendor to comfort him.

To Be Seen

When I was a kid,
I used to hold a TV remote
like a microphone
and interview myself in the mirror,
dreaming of someday making it big
as a writer or a singer
or an actor or a director
or a marine biologist or an eco-terrorist
or a massage therapist or a teacher
or a priest or a healer,
someone people care about.

Our little queer posse
started a ritual
for whenever someone gifted
us a teen bible meant to scrub
away the gay.
We drove around the countryside,
praising early YouTube stars and emo singers
and smoking cigarettes while tearing out psalms
and letting them fly out the window.

I bought my first car
with my own money,
hard-earned
from washing grease traps
and mopping dirty public restrooms,
plucking tampons off of walls,

and breaking down thirty-nine cardboard boxes every shift.
I sharpied   *fuck me, I'm a*
on the dash above the   *Celebrity*   emblem.
I'll be a shock rock star yet, bitches.

I thought I always wanted
to be someone's sick infatuation,
their dirty little secret
but now I want something different.
Real love is what I want
even though real love is real messy.
Real love is real talk
about wandering eyes and pornography
and failing intimacy tests
in the latest self-help magazines
even though you won't look up
from the word game on your smartphone.
Will you look at me
when I am talking to you?

Please.

Drought

Third set of human remains found at Lake Mead amid drought
– CNN headline from July 27, 2022

We are in yet another dry spell

       passion lost and passion parched

and remnants keep popping up
in the murky mud
as the water recedes

lost plastic dolls and missing report cards
love letters and rusted heart-shaped lockets
human remains and wrecked boats
relics from a peopled past

       and as you continue to avoid touching me

   I wonder what will reveal itself next

Emergency Exit

When we first started dating, we created a jingle parody:
The best part of waking up is my dick in your butt.
We laughed in bed, him nuzzling himself against my erection.
And a part of me always wanted to be inside of him
while he held onto my arm wrapped around him tight;
as if by he holding me inside
I knew he was not going to abandon me in the night.

Now, I notice that regardless of the temperature,
he sleeps with one foot uncovered
as if he always needs to be prepared to make a quick escape.

Pop Quiz

Name _____   Score _____/10 pts

_____ 1. How many siblings do I have? (1 pt)
        a. one
        b. two
        c. three
        d. four

_____ 2. What was the make and model of my first car? (1 pt)
        a. VW Beetle
        b. Chevrolet Impala
        c. Geo Metro
        d. Chevrolet Celebrity

_____ 3. Who is my favorite musician? (1 pt)
        a. Melissa Etheridge
        b. Moby
        c. Mandy Moore
        d. Madonna

_____ 4. What color are my eyes? (1 pt)
        a. the color of honey
        b. the color of Mississippi mud
        c. the color of swirled cotton candy
        d. the colors of the sea

_____ 5. What way would I rather die? (1 pt)
  a. burn
  b. bleed
  c. drown
  d. ~~fall~~ fly

6. Why am I not worthy of love? Write a claim with sufficient
   support. (5 pts)

Extraction

One of my wisdom teeth
grew in completely sideways,
causing damage
to the tooth next to it.

I understand what that's like.

Wait, there's a better metaphor –

I keep racing around the same track
over and over and over again,
creating deep marks into the dirt raceway.
It's easy to veer into these grooves,
sing the same song,
stuck making the same circles
when the destination
is eighteen hundred miles west of here.

Wait, there's a better metaphor –

I am a child reaching for a glass of milk or the needle
but the glasses keep getting put up on higher and higher shelves
and the needles litter this roach-infested apartment floor.
The needle becomes a path,
a friend.

And in it all, love, you are the innocent straight-standing tooth,
the one trying to smooth out these tracks,

the one trying to hum a song of salvation,
the one who reaches for the glass
but I keep choosing the familiar road to rage.

And I think that's enough metaphors.

I think it's time you remove what causes you such pain.

Drowning in Dreamland

& we are at a fancy fundraiser
& we have been fighting
but i am all fake smiles
& he won't fake it at all.

we silently fight
& i keep pushing his hand away
when his fingertips desperately reach out for mine.
i shake the hand of an acquaintance
& stir up casual conversation
about the mayor's facelift
& yo-yo diets
& what-have-you.

& he disappears
but keeps coming back
until he doesn't.
& then i begin to wonder
if he's snuck out on the patio
to smoke even though we promised each other
we wouldn't smoke anymore.

later i get a message delivered to me
& it says that he had swallowed a bunch of pills
because he didn't think i loved him anymore
& i probably had one hour until it was too late.

it was a game to find him

& prove my love.

he was trying to get back at me for my honesty
about wanting another's touch
& he always liked long baths
so i figured that's where he would be.

i called on a couple of the servants to discreetly
help me search all the bathrooms in this mansion.

& we started on the ground floor
& found diplomats snorting nose candy
& ranchers with their stable boys' cocks inside
& politicians applying more coverup
& the tubs were all gleaming
& empty
& we were racing the clock.
we worked our way up to the second floor
& the third
& nothing.
nothing.
nothing
& the one maid had a noticeable birthmark
like a tiger had slashed her face.
she wondered
about the basement
where the servants slept when needed for extended stays.

& we rushed down golden stairways
& through the kitchen
& down the less-pretty basement stairwell

& into the less-pretty basement level
that resembled interrogation cells in a john grisham thriller movie
& we tried one bathroom.
& then the next.
& then the next.
& then the next
& then there he was slumped
& pale in lukewarm water
up to his belly button.

& he had the smuggest smirk on his face.

& this was just a game to him.
& i was done with the games.
i yanked him onto the cold tiled floor
& i breathed my life into him
& i told him that was the last thing
he would ever get from me.
i was done.
done.
done.

& i think the tiger woman called an ambulance
but i did not stay to find out.

Zombie

Every morning,
I used to send positive text messages
to my closest friends:
inspirational quotes and images
and videos of me dancing in the bathroom mirror;
hoping to bring a little sugar
to these bitter days.

Lately,
I have stopped texting people.
I have stopped calling.
I stopped singing.
I stopped laughing.
I stopped masturbating.
I started picking at old scabs.

I now lay in a grave
of matching pillowcases
stuffed with mismatched pillows
waiting for someone who loved me
to show me love in the present tense,
waiting for someone to resurrect this dead thing.

In the Company of Ghosts

After seventy-four days of stumbling
over the box of shit he left at my place,
I decide it's time to throw it out.

But first, I torment myself
by going through these leftover relics
one more time.

It's for closure, I try to fool myself.
But I'm not buying it. I know myself too well.
I'm too fond of fingering a bloody wound.

I toss out his crappy pop CDs
but keep a few of the good ones.
I toss out his Clone-a-Willy silicone copy of my dick.

I throw out his sketchpad and junk mail.
I don't throw out his tax folder.
(I'm not a monster.)

And then I come to a manilla envelope
full of evidence and theories about the ghosts
he has encountered on his journeys.

I wonder if there's a guiding spirit
who lives in this house,
a friendly ghost who gave him company.

A friend who helped him see
the courage he harbored inside to move on
from me and into his own happiness.

I wonder if it's weird
that I want to become this ghost's friend, too.
Is it weird to befriend your ex's ghoul?

Let's dig out this dusty spirit board and see
if ghosts can cure loneliness and heartache.

Mourning the Dead Cat

The cat died and my dog
does not know how to cope.

She walks around distraught
and anytime she finds a piece of cat hair,

she sniffs it. She inhales too deeply
and she lets out a great sneeze.

And though I always try to stop her,
she chooses to eat the dead cat's hair

as if to say, *Hey, Sister,*
you will live in me now.

I will carry you.

. . .

Atlas of Longing

It is 59 miles to the mall.
It is 133 miles for a vegan restaurant.
It is 123 miles to the nearest gay bar.
It is 145 miles averaged for a decent concert.
It is 21 miles to buy a lube that's any good for butt stuff.
271 miles to witness the Dalai Lama's wisdom.
497 miles traveled to hear Joy Harjo read.
1,692 miles to where my first boyfriend lived.
20 miles to where my first *real* boyfriend lived.
20 miles to where my first real boyfriend kissed me.

21 miles to where my first real boyfriend raped me with massage
      oil as lubricant.
682 miles I moved to be closer to the first Brandon I loved.
0 miles I had to travel to fuck my first Brandon. Not the one I
      loved.
746 miles moved with the second Brandon I loved, the third gay
      Brandon overall.
23 miles from where my abuser lives.
22 miles from where my abuser works.
0 miles from where my abuser lurks.

And it is 633 miles to the mountains.
It is 1,117 miles to the desert.
It is 1,467 miles to the Atlantic Ocean.
It is 1,852 miles to the Pacific.
It is 33,900,000 miles to Mars.
93,000,000 miles to the Sun.

And cataloging all these miles,
rough and smooth,
past and future maybes add up to something:
it'll take bravery and some wild life choices to find my way back to
      joy.

Acknowledgments

Thank you to these literary journals and presses who originally published versions of the following pieces sometimes with different titles:

& Change: "Drought" "His Holy Trinity"
Chapter House Journal: "Just in Case"
Door is a Jar Magazine: "Roadside Assistance"
Emerge Literary Journal: "Flying in Dreamland"
Fifth Wheel Press: "On Creation"
One Art: "Barter" "In Response to *Alex* (Pencil & Oil Pastels, 2007)"
Resurrection Magazine: "One Last Polka"
Sage Cigarettes: "Howl"
Snowflake Magazine: "Atlas of Longing" "In the Company of Ghosts"
Stone Pacific Zine: "Cloudy Fragments (Notes App After Hookup on May 3, 2022)", "Christening," and "Anything But"
The Storms: "Mourning the Dead Cat"
Tilted House: "Quarantine Lovers"
Unstamatic: "Zombie"

The final line in "Christening" references a line in "Song of Myself" by Walt Whitman.

"His Holy Trinity (And He Says, 'Oh God')" takes inspiration from "Footnote to Howl" by Allen Ginsberg.

An earlier version of "Lit in Dreamland" was shortlisted for *Litro Magazine's* Surreal and Strange: Prose Poetry Competition.

"To Be Seen" utilizes a lyric from the song "Lollipop Luxury" by
Jeffree Star. The author acknowledges Star's problematic actions
and does not condone such behavior.

Brandon Carter, thank you for your love.

Aurora Bones, thank you for your insight.

Sammi Stange, thank you for being a friend.

Sven Davisson and Rebel Satori, thank you for for your dedication.

About the Author

Charles K. Carter (they/he) is a queer poet from Iowa who currently lives in Oregon. They share their home with their artist husband and their spoiled pets. He enjoys film, yoga, and live music. Melissa Etheridge is their ultimate obsession. Carter holds an MFA in writing from Lindenwood University. His poems have appeared in numerous literary journals. They are the author of *If the World Were a Quilt* (Kelsay Books) and *Read My Lips* (David Robert Books) as well as several chapbooks.

www.CKCpoetry.com